Michaels
THE ARTS AND CRAFTS STORE®

GARDEN STYLE

Michaels
THE ARTS AND CRAFTS STORE®

GARDEN STYLE

beautiful
How the Fashion Stars Live

contents

introduction

Let your imagination soar as Michaels helps you create stylish and personal designs for your garden and for the inside of your home.

Enhance your home with a unique charm and ambiance that blends the comforts of indoor living with the serenity of the outdoors. *Michaels Garden Style* shows you how to capture the rich yet casual feeling that makes the indoor-outdoor approach to decorating so popular today. With this collection of gorgeous photographs of Michaels products, expert advice, and special tips, you'll see how easy it is to create harmony between indoor and outdoor living spaces. Plus, we'll show you lots of ideas for using decorative items in unexpected ways. Let *Michaels Garden Style* inspire your own decorating ideas, too. Use it as a starting point for adding personal touches and artistic flair to your designs. If you're ready to bring a little more sunshine, fresh air, and flowers into your life, all you have to do is turn the page and get started!

COSMOS
WELCOME

1

plant stands

Today, the lines separating indoor and outdoor living spaces are blurring. Was it in the Garden of Eden that our love affair with open-air rooms began? Perhaps, but wherever or whenever it happened, the romance of a classic light-filled conservatory and the charm of a pretty patio or porch continues to cast a spell. Much of the allure of such places comes from lush potted plants displayed on graceful tables, pedestals, and stands. Objects of utility, plant stands are also highly decorative, so it is not surprising that designers love to use them in place of conventional indoor side tables and occasional tables, as well as

Use plant stands as unique accent furniture.

for displaying plants. Placed next to the front door, a plant stand is a handy spot for the mail or keys; in the living room, it can be a place to set a drink; in the bedroom, it can substitute as a nightstand; in the bath, it can hold towels, soaps, or toiletries. A variety of shapes, sizes, styles, and finishes make plant stands instantly at home anywhere!

beautiful
How the Fashion Stars Live

Design Hint

Make your indoor garden rooms truly seasonal by changing the plants to reflect the different times of the year. Use bulb plants such as daffodils, tulips, or hyacinths in the spring; miniature roses, zinnias, or geraniums in the summer; and chrysanthemums in the fall. Brighten up winter with forced bulbs, such as paperwhites or amaryllis, or hold to tradition with pointsettias and flowering Christmas cacti.

This pretty plant stand, opposite, placed next to an old iron bed, has an antiqued finish that reinforces the vintage look of the room. In a stand this size, you can easily fit one or two potted plants. You might want to choose one plant for color and one for scent.

The leaf-patterned tile atop the plant stand, above and above right, adds texture to a simple design. The stand is the perfect size for a small wall where it serves handsomely as a petite table next to a door.

Available at Michaels: ***Antiqued plant stand*** • ***Flower pots*** • ***Tile-top plant stand***

GET DECORATING

There are numerous ways to use plant stands to introduce a variety of shapes, heights, materials, and textures to a room to make it more interesting visually. For example, use a metal plant stand to counterbalance the wood furniture in a room. If the other pieces are rectilinear in shape, choose a plant stand that has curves. Do the opposite if the other tables in the room are oval or round. In this case, add a square or rectangular plant stand. Take it a step further: use a plant stand with a tile top to bring color or pattern into a room that is essentially neutral or plain. And don't forget—plants add color, too.

Design Hint

Design professionals always include some greenery in their rooms. Plants are like natural works of art; they are colorful, shapely, and evocative. Large plants are dramatic, but not everyone has a home that can accommodate a large ficus tree or a tall, graceful palm. A small plant on a tall stand may be the solution. Another thing you can do is mass several plants together in a tiered arrangement on stands of varying heights or use one plant stand with several tiers. For added height, try placing a plant on a pedestal or stand behind another plant that's on the floor. Finally, use accent lighting. What could be more theatrical than the shadow play of leaves or fronds cast on a wall by aiming a small spotlight upwards from underneath a bold, sculptural plant? Palms are excellent for creating this effect.

The look of weathered metal adds Old World charm to this plant stand, opposite top, especially when it's paired with an urn and statuary.

A three-tiered plant stand, opposite bottom, is a pretty accent piece placed in front of an antique metal tile.

An elegant tabletop stand, above left, elevates a small potted plant, creating an interesting arrangement of items of various sizes.

A grouping of several stands, right, fills out a plain corner in a room without crowding it. Note the decorative detail of the top of the stand, above right.

Available at Michaels: ***All plant stands • Clay pots • Reclining angel • Urn planter • Finials***

ADD COLOR ACCENTS

One of the hottest trends today is garden-style decorating, so you can see how perfectly attractive plant stands can play a role in your home's decor. Keep in mind that in addition to the stand itself, the color of the plants that you are displaying is important, too. Try to find flowering houseplants that coordinate with the room's color scheme. Look for ones that match, harmonize with, or contrast with other furnishings in the room. If you're not blessed with a green thumb or if you simply want to liven up a room that doesn't receive adequate light, don't be afraid to create your arrangement using artificial plants. Many silk designs can fool all but the most discerning eye.

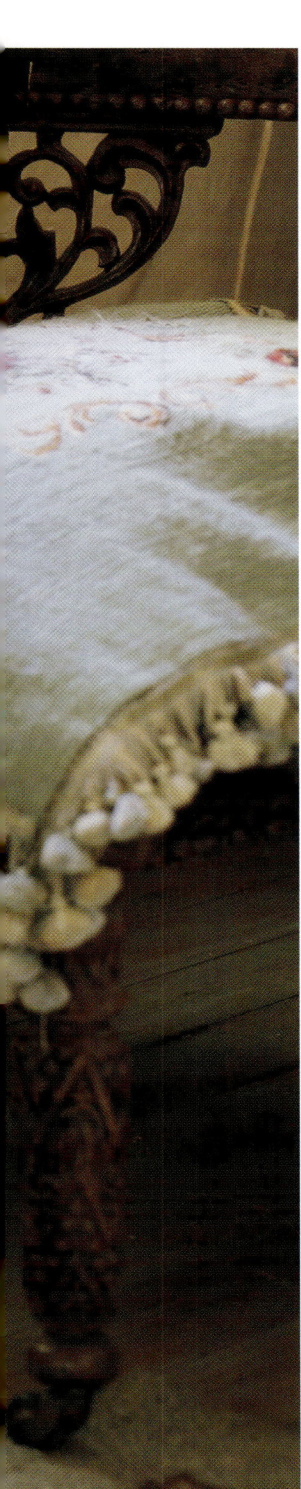

A three-tiered plant stand in off white, opposite, strikes a sweet pose. The potted pink cyclamen, a seasonal plant, is actually artificial. The rosy petals pick up the color of the posies on the stitched chair cushion. When you want to make a change, this lightweight stand folds easily for storage.

The top of the plant stand, above and in profile above left, features a glazed mosaic-tile finish and handpainted flowers. Here it lightens up an otherwise traditional interior.

Available at Michaels: ***Plant stands*** • ***Artificial plants***

The look of old tiles, left, has an earthy, texturous quality to it. Like its clay inspiration, this plant stand's surface is practical for its ability to withstand drips and spills from just-watered and misted plants.

Gathering several plants on and around a low, small stand, opposite, allows them to bask in the morning sunlight and spring air through a door left ajar.

Available at Michaels: ***Tile-top plant stand*** • ***Clay pots***

Design Hint

Sucessfully matching plants to room conditions can mean the difference between a healthy plant and one that you'll have to throw away after a short time. Temperature, light, and humidity are key factors that vary from daytime to nighttime and from room to room. An entry is prone to drafts and may be short on natural light, for example. So choose your plants accordingly. Good candidates for an entry or hallway include: aspidistra, begonia; spider plant; dieffenbachia; dracaena; ficus; prayer plant; philodendron; and arrowhead vine.

ARTFUL STORAGE

Bringing garden style indoors can be achieved with or without plants. Don't forget: plant stands can be used in many ways. For example, use a plant stand to display handsome clay pots. Stack them or line them up side by side. Accent the display with other items from the garden such as small statuary, balls of twine, or even small garden tools. For impact: create a vignette of like items. Group several sizes of galvanized pails or watering cans on a plant stand, or make an arrangement with your collection of bird houses. Use your imagination!

CREATIVE IDEA

Pedestals of any kind can make fabulous plant stands. Paired with an aged clay pot, right, this one easily makes the transition from house to garden. If you don't have an old clay pot to go with your pedestal, create one. There are a couple of easy ways to add instant age to terra-cotta. If you have leftover garden lime, make a paste of it by adding a little water. Then scrub it onto the pot with an old brush. Let it dry to a soft, white finish. Over time, the growth of natural mold will enhance the patina. Another way to age a clay pot is with something right out of the refrigerator—yogurt. Use a clean cloth to rub the yogurt onto the pot, and then leave the pot in a damp place until mold grows.

These three plant stands, opposite, are of similar scale with slight variations in style and finish.

A hand-painted porcelain Chinese garden seat, opposite below, can be a work of art on its own or serve as a plant stand. The coordinating umbrella stand makes a pretty vase here.

Curlicues and flourishes embellish this plant stand, right, with Victorian style. It's as charming in the garden as it would be on a patio, porch, or any indoor room.

The look of antique ironwork and an "aged patina" bring classic style to this petite plant stand, right, and to the one pictured below.

Available at Michaels: ***All plant stands • Faux ceramic and terra-cotta decorative flower pots • Clay pots • Chinese hand-painted porcelain garden seat and umbrella stand • Upholstered footstool***

2

plant containers

As soon as the weather turns warm, avid gardeners love to roll up their sleeves and plunge into their favorite pastime. But even if you can't tell a petunia from a pansy and the thought of spending an afternoon elbow deep in compost leaves you cold, you can still turn to garden-style decorating to enhance all of your outdoor and indoor living areas.

Begin by picking out some different plant containers from the dozens of styles available. You'll find the old standbys, but you will also discover containers in sizes, shapes, and materials that may be unfamiliar to you and different from what you

Use containers to transform your deck or patio.

usually see at garden centers. Don't stop there, though. You'll get more value while adding some of your own personality to the design by thinking of different ways of using these items. Start by using some of these containers in the kitchen and bathroom, or fill a shallow one with potpourri. From there you will discover dozens of other uses.

FOR GARDENERS

Select plant containers that complement the plant's appearance and growing habits. Bushy, round plants often look best in bowl- or dish-shaped pots. Tall plants look best in cylindrical containers. And don't forget that the container has to accommodate the plant's root system. Some plants have shallow roots; others have deep-growing ones. A plant with an extensive root system needs a tall container, while a plant with few roots needs only a shallow container to thrive.

Design Hint

When growing potted plants on windowsills, tabletops, or other furniture, be sure to protect the surfaces from water stains. You can buy plastic trays or saucers to place under the pots. If you are using clay pots, use matching saucers. But if the saucers are unglazed, water may still seep through. In these cases, rest the pot and saucer on a cork or felt protector.

An old sink, opposite, holds a variety of plant containers and garden accessories while making an attractive display on this patio. Home gardeners require pots of different sizes and shapes, top. A weathered-finish terrarium might be used as a planter, or it could be used to display garden ornaments or decorative plates as shown above.

A copper-finish plant container, right, commands attention in the corner of this porch. Place containers like this on old tables, footstools, or plant stands that you can purchase.

Available at Michaels: ***Green metal vase • Clay pots (12 in. and smaller) • Galvanized watering can • White porcelain vase • Silk flowers • Terrarium • Copper-finish planter***

Mixing natural and artificial plants, top and above, provides flexibility in creating dramatic presentations. You can also change them whenever you wish.

When creating a grouping, center, be sure to include containers of different sizes and shapes for the best effect. Use hanging items, opposite top, and tall, colorful items, opposite middle, as well.

Large baskets, opposite bottom, make great places to store small planters and other garden items.

Available at Michaels: ***Tall white bucket • Small galvanized bucket • Clay pots • Silk flowers • Wheat grass • Wire tricycle basket • Large galvanized bucket • Tan basket • Metal crosses • Plant stand with tile top • Red bucket vase • Grapevine basket • Wall container***

Design Hint

There are many hanging plant containers available, such as the one shown at top right. But for a different look, try converting an ordinary floor or tabletop model to a hanging one. Support the container with L-shaped brackets, or drill holes through the back of the container and fasten it to the wall using screws and washers. When attaching the container to drywall, use the proper hollow-wall anchors.

OPEN-AIR ROOMS

A backyard barbecue, a late-afternoon tea in the conservatory, or a candlelit dinner on the patio can all be special occasions. Make the most of them by creating your outdoor rooms to suit your style of entertaining. Many people locate a casual eating area behind the house, removed from the scrutiny of passersby. Decorate the patio or deck with plants placed in colorful plant containers. Remember to choose containers that show off the plants to their best advantage.

A hanging planter, left, is teamed up with a decorative tabletop plant container.

Festive tables, above and opposite, get their start with lots of flowering plants. If you are using all cut flowers, mix the container sizes for visual variety.

Available at Michaels: ***Hanging wire planter • Daisy planter • Clay pots • Silk flowers • Tall metal vase • Galvanized bucket • Galvanized tray with faux finish • Glazed porcelain plant stand, vase, and mug***

Design Hint

Don't just fill those plant containers with plants. As shown in the photos above and right, you can fill mugs and ceramic vases with bread sticks, use them to hold fruits or berries, or turn a plant stand into a serving piece. Line a metal container with a tea towel, and place silverware and napkins in it. Fill an elongated metal plant container with crushed ice, and pack it with beverages. The ice will melt, of course, but the makeshift cooler will make your life easier when you need to serve many drinks during a short period of time.

CREATING STYLE

If you yearn for a personal outdoor retreat, it does not matter where you live, nor is the size of your property or budget that important. What's important is that you rely on your personal style to create your oasis. Complete plans for your design by including plant containers that fit well with the overall style of your yard or garden. These accessories can help tie your design plans together.

CREATIVE IDEA

Garden-style design is a loose, casual look that evokes a laid-back feeling. This gives you a great deal of flexibility when planning gardens, patios, and decks. But take it further: bring the same casual attitude indoors by adapting garden elements for inside the house. The wall container, right, is an example of adaptive use. Rather than using the container to hold plants on a wall or fence, bring it indoors and fill it with magazines and newspapers. You can also use it to hold mail or written messages you want to leave for your family. Place a few containers in the kitchen to hold dried herbs. Hang one near the front entry, and fill it with fresh-cut or dried flowers.

Wall buckets, opposite, are great for growing herbs. Place a series of them near the kitchen door so that the herbs will be close at hand when you're cooking.

Tabletop presentations, above, are focal points. Choose a variety of items for the design. The copper-finish watering can, right, can be part of the setting.

Available at Michaels: ***Hanging wall containers*** • ***Tall bucket*** • ***Shallow elongated bucket*** • ***Faux-painted pots*** • ***Wire tricycle container*** • ***Clay pots*** • ***Wheat grass*** • ***Silk flowers*** • ***Copper-finish watering can***

3

garden statuary

The careful selection and artful placement of a few well-chosen treasures personalizes and finishes off an outdoor area like nothing else can. Whether you decide on placing a birdbath at the center of an herb garden or creating a grand arrangement of sculpture in a more formal garden, you and your visitors will welcome these landing spots to break up areas of foliage or lawn, wall, or walkway. After all, an inviting landscape and outdoor living environment is more than just plants and structures.

Archaeological evidence suggests that people have been adorning their outdoor spaces with

Decorative accessories add personality to your yard.

decorative objects for centuries, whether as an offering to a deity or for purely aesthetic reasons. Today, you can find a variety of statuary to accessorize and personalize your outdoor living rooms, patios, decks, and porches. You can create a formal look or simply add some of your own personality to an outdoor space.

ADD SPARKLE

Color is a dynamic tool that is often overlooked when adding statuary and other accessories to a yard or garden. But the use of color can have a great effect on garden design. A splash of color can serve as a unifying element, bringing harmony to a group of items, or it can be the focal point of the garden. When introducing color, begin by placing a few items at first to avoid overwhelming an area. You can always add more later.

The patio setting, opposite, combines colorful statuary with potted plants. Change plants to fit the season.

The mosaic rabbit, top left, adds a spark of color whether placed on the patio or in the garden.

The swirls of the finial, top right, echo a classic garden ornament design.

The mosaic turtle, above left, can be used on its own or with other colorful statues.

Available at Michaels: ***Mosaic rabbit*** • ***Finial with swirl texture*** • ***Mosaic turtle*** • ***Clay pots***

Design Hint

Choosing the right statue or accessory for the right place is the key to a successful arrangement of items in your yard or garden. The item should be in scale with its environment. A small accessory set by itself in a large space will be dwarfed by its surroundings. However, a petite statue becomes a treasured detail when it is tucked into a small gap between two stones. Or group a number of small items together to create a larger scene in the garden. In contrast, a large statue needs a place of importance. Use one as the focal point at the end of a long pathway or set in the corner of the yard.

CREATE A DESIGN

There are no hard-and-fast rules about what to use to decorate the garden. It's all a matter of taste, and you can feel free to experiment with various items. Do you want to make a bold statement that you might not feel right about expressing inside the house? Nature itself is grand, so don't be timid when selecting objects. Bear in mind that something that looks huge in a small shop may be too small in proportion to your outdoor room.

Should your outdoor decoration be formal or informal in style? It's hard to draw the line sometimes. Formal gardens are based on geometry, and as such they are orderly and organized. In a traditional or formal garden, just the placement of objects can create symmetry and add a sense of scale. Although not always true, an informal garden tends to appear less planned and studied. Loose, asymmetrical arrangements of items in a cottage or country garden underscore the casual mood.

The resin fairy, opposite, can adorn a garden bench, as shown here, or be grouped with similar figures. You can either choose statues that are all the same size or mix sizes.

The poly-foam wall planter and resin reclining angel, right, are used here to create a unique scene or setting in the garden. You can make such a scene the focal point of your yard or garden, or tuck it in an out-of-the-way corner.

Angel statues, such as this pair at left, are becoming more and more popular. Use them to decorate a garden, porch, or patio, or place them just inside a front or rear entrance to your home.

Available at Michaels: ***Resin fairy*** • ***Wall plant container*** • ***Resin reclining angel*** • ***Twin resin angels***

Design Hint

Selecting garden statuary based on one or two themes tends to have more of an impact than picking a number of dissimilar items and placing them in the garden or yard.

Design Hint

Placement is everything when arranging statues. Some elements are best sitting by themselves. Others are better when they are part of a larger grouping.

The birdbath, left, is supported by a trio of frogs.

The tabletop birdbath, above, will work on any water-resistant surface.

Add personality to a garden, right, by grouping statues.

The small garden seat, below right, offers an inscription.

This pineapple birdbath, left, is one of many designs available.

A rain chime, far left, brings music to the yard.

Available at Michaels: ***Frog birdbath • Tabletop birdbath • Angel rain chime • Pineapple birdbath • Twin angels • Reclining angel • Garden seat with inscription***

ADDING PERSONALITY

Just like the accessories you arrange inside your home to complement your decorating style, the things that adorn your exterior spaces reflect your unique personality. Whatever your garden style is—formal, traditional, rustic, refined, or a combination of them all—don't be afraid to go with your instincts when choosing and arranging objects of artful whimsy. Let your outdoor rooms reflect your style. For a pleasing arrangement, always defer to the principles of scale and proportion, balance, harmony, and line.

The miniature wheelbarrow, above left, looks best when grouped with similar items.

The resin frog, above, offers the chance to inject some humor into your garden.

A plaster-like resin medallion, left, provides a message of welcome to anyone who sees it.

Arrange garden accessories indoors, far right, to create truly distinctive decorating.

This resin artichoke finial, right, is one of many finial statue designs offered by Michaels.

GARDEN HUMOR

A touch of humor adds to the overall pleasure of the garden. Even in a formal landscape, there is room for a subtle joke or even some broad humor.

Don't worry if you can't tell a joke. All you need is a childlike enthusiasm for things that are funny—or even things that are just plain silly—to select the right garden accessories. For example, there are a variety of animals available like the frog shown above that will coax a smile out of anyone. You can either place it in plain sight or, for even more impact, conceal it behind some plants so that someone will discover it by accident.

Available at Michaels: ***Resin wheelbarrow • Sitting frog • Welcome medallion • Acorn finial • Ceramic bowl • Hanging plant container (with magazines) • Terrarium and ornaments • Poly-foam urn • Artichoke finial***

CREATIVE IDEA

Some items look as good indoors as they do outside. Place this double-handled ceramic bowl on a sunny window sill and fill it with moss or small stones. Group it with other items as shown here and to the right.

4

garden arches

Adding a garden arch to your yard makes a bold visual statement. Not only do garden arches provide a place to grow climbing plants, giving your yard a vertical landscaping component, they add a distinctive architectural accent to your garden as well. Using a few in tandem can convey a sense of enclosure, especially if they're covered in foliage.

Garden arches command attention, so plan carefully where you place them. Use arches to frame a garden path, or place one at the entrance to your garden. Many people use garden arches to signal a change of function between parts of their yard. You might place one between a play area and a formal garden, for example. And don't forget to include the arches in your holiday decorating plans. Or you could make the arch itself a destination within the yard. Place seating beneath an arch or arches and add lighting, and you'll have a personal getaway right in your own backyard.

The airy designs of arches add elegance to your yard.

FOCAL POINTS

Focal points attract your attention. They are the first thing you see when you enter the yard; they become your destination when you stroll through the garden. To create a garden arch focal point, place it along a garden path, in a corner of the yard, or in any prominent location.

The wind chime, above, provides a nice accent to the peak in this arch. Other possible accessories include the decorative Chinese seat and gold-colored planter, above right.

A garden arch, right and opposite, commands the attention of anyone in the yard. The bench, decorative accessories, and location of the arch make it a destination in this garden.

Available at Michaels: ***Mediterranean garden arch* • *Wind chime* • *Hand-painted porcelain Chinese garden seat* • *Golden planter***

The wedding arch, right, will help make any couple's wedding day a memorable experience. Place it at the entrance of a garden to make a welcoming statement, or set up a few to line a garden path. Decorate with garland or tulle, below, or look for silk flowers that complement the bridal bouquet.

The classic green arch, opposite, frames the entrance to a home for a special occasion. This arch can provide good support for lightweight climbing vines or roses. An alternative is to decorate it with garland and silk flowers. Complete the landscaping by placing potted plants at its base.

Available at Michaels:
Wedding arch • Grapevine silk garland • Tulle • Planting urns • Green arch

SPECIAL OCCASIONS

Adding a temporary garden arch or decorating an existing one can help you celebrate the special times in your life, such as birthdays, weddings, graduations, and anniversaries. Plant climbing plants for year-round decoration, or decorate the arch with silk flowers, garland, or fabrics to change its appearance whenever you like. And don't forget to decorate garden arches for the holidays that are special to you.

Design Hint

There are many ways to decorate a garden arch, including the ones shown in this book. If you are going to complete the arch with plants, be sure to select ones that will thrive in your climate zone. Also, make sure that the arch is strong enough to support the type of plant you pick. Proceed by placing the arch where you want it, and then observe the amount of sun it receives throughout the day. The personnel at a good garden center or your local extension agent should be able to recommend the right plants to place around your garden arch.

CREATIVE IDEA

Little details can make or break any design. Use the metal accessories shown right and far right to complete borders and planting beds. Place the large ladybug and bee among shrubs in a perennial border. The butterfly and mushrooms look great in planters, alongside walks, and in window boxes.

CREATIVE IDEA

After you've lived with your garden lights for a while, replace all of the gel candles with lights of different colors. You will be surprised how the change in accent enhances the look of your yard.

LIGHT TOUCHES

Add another dimension to your yard or garden, and get more use out of it, as well, by installing decorative lighting. Start by covering a garden arch with small decorative lights. You can use multicolor lights or, for a more sophisticated look, use single-color strands or "blankets." Supplement the arch lights with lanterns and torches. When selecting lights, pick those that look as good during the day as they do at night.

A lighted arch, opposite and left, can help your yard come alive at night. The arch is covered in a "blanket" of small, decorative outdoor lights. The gel torches can be placed where you need them. The arch is the centerpiece of this yard, but you can place a number of arches along a path to create a stunning visual effect. The hanging lantern, above, holds a votive candle and works with almost any garden design.

Available at Michaels: ***White arch* • *Decorative light blanket* • *Gel torches* • *Metal ladybug and bee* • *Butterfly pick* • *Porcelain mushrooms* • *Hanging lantern***

5

decorative metalwork

Metal art is one of the easiest ways to add panache or a whimsical note to an outdoor area or a garden-style room. If you've admired the way that designers are decorating with vintage ornamental metalwork today, you'll be delighted to know that you can do the same. It doesn't have to be expensive, either, if you stay out of trendy salvage yards and shy away from pricey antique shops. Attractive interpretations of the old-fashioned iron grilles, gates, window guards, balconies, and fences that proliferated during the nineteenth century are now available in affordable, lightweight designs. Some

Metal ornament is perfect for home and garden.

of them even reflect the details that distinguished the various works of artisans in different regions of the country. In Boston, for example, patterns often featured classical themes such as urns, spears, laurels, or the Greek key motif, while in the South, floral designs flourished. Take your pick. Metal art makes a great accent piece anywhere.

A series of twisted double "C" scrolls make up this design, left. You can see a detail of the scrollwork, above. On an exterior wall, this plaque adds an attractive vertical element to a plain wall. In addition, it can camouflage imperfections in a wall. This design is suitable for indoor use, or you can use it outdoors in a sheltered area if you want to preserve the frame.

Hammered metal leaves and flowers, above center and right, are two of the most popular motifs found on decorative metal accessories like this grapevine trellis.

Terra-cotta pots filled with colorful blossoms draw attention to this striking wall-mounted plant holder, opposite top and right. Classic details, such as the lion's head relief on the metal tiles, the fleur-de-lis at the top, and the ribbon-end scrolls, add distinction.

Available at Michaels: ***Framed "C" scroll wall piece* • *Hammered-leaf trellis* • *Metal lion's head plant holder* • *Clay pots***

LOOK FOR INSPIRATION

How many times has something pretty caught your eye, but you've said to yourself, "Where would I put it?" There are lots of places to look for inspiration. Start here, and keep going: you can find additional ideas for using these popular metal accent pieces in all kinds of ways by checking out the latest decorating magazines. Plus, don't forget about all of the wonderful show houses and garden tours that take place during the spring. For a modest entrance fee, which typically goes to charity, you can spend a morning or an afternoon observing what professional designers are doing. You'll see lots of examples of decorative metal, because it's a classic material that's practical and ornamental at the same time. It's versatile, too. Use it as a centerpiece or as a detail that supports your overall theme.

Design Hint

Keep your eyes open when you walk on the beach, in the woods, or through the fields. The well-trained eye can spot "garden ornaments" almost anywhere to complement traditional metalwork. Holiday excursions are an excellent time for a scavenger hunt that may uncover an interesting addition for your garden that is also a souvenir. Here are some suggestions: abandoned birds' nests and feathers; interesting rocks; driftwood and seashells; or vintage bottles.

EXTRAORDINARIES

Fragments of old architectural or metal ornament are highly sought after by collectors today for embellishing their homes with found "objets d'art." But you don't have to go to auctions or antique markets to get the same look. The fabulous "finds" pictured here only look vintage. Outdoors, they'll help you create a special corner in your yard. Indoors, combine one or several pieces with pretty floral fabrics, pottery, framed botanical prints, and an arrangement of seasonal silk flowers. Add a basket of heavenly scented potpourri or perhaps a tabletop fountain, put on your favorite CD, sit back, and relax.

Acanthus leaves embellish the planter on a metal wall piece, opposite left.

Heart-shaped scrolls distinguish a metal trellis, opposite right, that's based on an old Charleston design.

Ribbed leaves swirl around heart-shaped scrolls to create an unusual work of art, opposite bottom.

A copper-finish wall shelf, right, makes a pretty display. An old bull's-eye window guard inspired the piece below. Another design, below far right, was based on an old sunflower motif.

Available at Michaels: ***All metal wall pieces • Metal stand • Silk flowers • Clay pots • Watering can***

Not your garden-variety insects, this tin ladybug and her tin bee buddy, above, add a playful note to a garden bed. Another tin critter, left, is one cool cat.

The fleur-de-lis garden stake, right, can be easily moved around the garden. Use it alone or paired with metal border stakes. Mount a matching metal planter, opposite left, to a wall or fence. The graceful metal butterfly trellis, opposite right, complements all of these items.

Available at Michaels: ***Tin ladybug, bee, and cat stakes • White iron fleur-de-lis stake • White iron border stakes • White iron planter • Butterfly trellis • Clay pot***

HAVE FUN WITH IT

Take time to smell the roses. There is nothing that says you have to be completely serious when you decorate, especially when it's a casual corner in your yard where you should expect to have fun. Whimsical items that are easy to move wherever you need an extra bit of color can also set the tone: "Hey this is a place where everybody plays, even the grownups!"

Design Hint

Make an interesting display in a garden with a lone peeling wooden shutter, a section of fencing, an old rusty bicycle, or a wobbly chair, to name a few ideas. In fact, even if an item has lost its luster, it can take on new life in the great outdoors. It can suddenly add invigorating new charm to a porch, patio, or garden room. So before you discard anything, remember that there may be lots of people waiting in line at the local garbage dump to take home your "junk."

6

mediterranean accents

Few people can live on the grand scale of having a villa in Italy or a manor house on the French Riviera. But you can capture the feeling of the Old World and the luscious landscapes, terraced gardens, and open-air courtyards of the Mediterranean with the right garden decor. Your interpretation should begin with an examination of your home's architecture and the landscaping around it. If the style of the house contains eighteenth- or early nineteenth-century features, such as a symmetrical placement of doors and windows, a stone or brick facade, and classical details, a few well-placed Mediterranean-inspired accessories will lend a bit of delightful informality to the mix. You can also use these decorative items to add character to a nondescript ranch house or a contemporary dwelling bereft of ornament or architectural embellishment. On the other hand, if you are a collector, some of the items featured here are based on antiques and may round out an eclectic art collection.

Add continental flair with Old World accents.

STYLE, AL FRESCO

The forerunners of the modern patio are the terraces and courtyards of grand European estates. Today, people want similar style and sophistication in their open-air rooms, but they prefer a less-formal setting for their comfort. One way to make the transition is by pairing casual wicker furniture with stylish accessories.

CREATIVE IDEA

A metal basket lined with sphagnum moss looks lush. After lining the basket, add planting soil. Ivy is a good plant choice. Thread the leaves through the openings, and then water. Keep the plant misted and out of the sun.

You can easily create your own Mediterranean fantasy in any outdoor space when you pull together the right furniture and details. Practical, durable faux wicker pieces, in natural, anchor this covered stone porch, opposite, and accessories punctuate the style.

Available at Michaels: ***Metal wire planter • Flowers and vase • Clay pot • Terrarium • Bird statuary***

Introduce a water element by nestling an enchanting birdbath, opposite far left, somewhere in your garden.

Reinforce your theme with a pineapple finial (a symbol of welcome), opposite bottom, a lion's head plaque, opposite middle, or a classical faux-stone wall pocket.

Scatter small decor items such as these water-bearing cherubs, right, to draw attention to various garden areas.

Available at Michaels: ***Birdbath • Foam wall pocket • Resin wall plaque • Resin pineapple finial • Wire basket • Water-bearing cherubs • Plastic planter • Clay pot***

Design Hint

Foam and plastic products mimic stone or clay, and they usually don't require indoor storage over the winter months.

An eclectic collection, above, makes an interesting display atop an old cupboard.

This antiqued cross, right, resembles an eighteenth-century French reliquary.

Metal and clay objects, left, have an earthy quality that evokes antiquity.

A container, opposite top, becomes artful with the addition of an ornate iron cross.

A stucco wall is the perfect backdrop for a collection of decorative crosses, opposite.

Available at Michaels: ***All crosses • Tall red container • Clay pots • Decorative metal container • Candles***

Design Hint

Play up Mediterranean-style decorating with paint. It's easy to make a surface look like aged stone. On a clean wall, first apply a base coat of warm white latex paint. Let it dry. Then, using a full-bodied flat latex base paint, create the desired stone color by adding taupe and beige artist's acrylics to warm white. Experiment with small quantities to determine the proportions. For a deeper, earthier hue, use an acrylic paint color that's closest to terra-cotta. Apply the mixed paint using a decorator's brush, pouncing and twisting the brush to create a stonelike texture.

Set the mood with color, left. Accent pieces play up Mediterranean style. A gorgeous arrangement of silk flowers coordinates with a striking ceramic vase and candles, below.

A wind chime, opposite top left, depicts the Mediterranean sun. The urn vase, opposite top right, captures Tuscany. A terrarium and little birds, opposite bottom left, and the faux-stone planter, opposite bottom right, resemble antiques.

Available at Michaels:
Ceramic and urn vases • Silk flowers • Candles • Basket • Clay pot • Wind chime • Urn planter • Terrarium • Bird statuary

INTERIOR DESIGNS

The secret to capturing the essence of any region is local color. What could be more reminiscent of the hills of Tuscany or the fields of Provence than their saturated hues? Think of vibrant yellow, intense blue, sun-ripened red, olive green, and earthy brown. These are the colors of the Mediterranean landscape, and they are as easily translatable inside your home as they are in the old farmhouses of the Italian and French countryside. Paint, fabric, and ceramic accessories are your tools. Tie your theme into the garden by incorporating a floral arrangement into your design.

7

garden lighting

Nothing will add as much magic to evenings spent outdoors in the garden or on your deck or patio than accent lighting. Strings of lights add a festive sparkle to any occasion. You can hang them from a tree, drape them along a fence or wall, or trim an outdoor umbrella with a rope of colorful party lights. Plug them into a nearby outdoor electrical receptacle, and you've got instant "atmosphere." Accentuate adorable topiaries with mini lights, too. Lighted novelty items are a great way to decorate, calling attention to a special feature or area. Use them all year-round; they even look pretty viewed from indoors. If you want ambiance

Set a mood with decorative lighting accents.

for outdoor entertaining, decorative torches in different sizes may be suitable for your tabletop, in a garden bed, around a pool, or next to the deck. Just move them anywhere you need them. Filled with citronella fuel, they may keep the bugs away, too. Combine outdoor lighting accents with in-ground lamps and lanterns for extra-special glamor.

A LITTLE ROMANCE

What is more conducive to relaxation and good times than soft light? Just as it can indoors, the right glow will make everything—the garden, the food, and you—look scrumptious. Layer the effect with candles, strings of minature lights, and torches. Install lights at varying heights: hang strings high up in tall tree branches as well as amid low shrubs. Weave light strings in and out of a trellis or around columns. Use charming novelty lights to create a theme that you can play out with other accessories having similar motifs.

Design Hint

Besides having pretty things to look at in your garden room, you need pleasant sounds for the overall ambiance to be complete. A small musical accent such as a wind chime or a bell hanging from a tree branch may provide that one extra pleasing note that will delight your senses.

Tableptop bamboo torches, opposite, with gel torches and festive string lights (page 70) in the planted beds, are great for outdoor parties. The glow bug on the tree adds whimsey.

Miniature lights enliven shapes and forms, such as the grapevine frog (with umbrella), top left, and topiary, middle left.

Some large garden torches, such as the type at left, can be lit with citronella fuel or kerosene. Others use gel candles, right.

Create a conversation corner, top, with tall bamboo torches and a glowing potted flower for added decorative fun.

Available at Michaels: ***Tabletop and large garden torches*** • ***Glow bug*** • ***String lights*** • ***Lighted frog, topiary, and potted flower*** • ***Wind chime*** • ***Multicolored gel torches***

Lighted dragonflies, flowers, and frogs, left and opposite, are made of wire and accented with colorful beads for a festive mood. Nestled amid plants and shrubs, right top and middle, the adorable creatures sparkle in the dense greenery.

The animated, lighted tortoise and flamingo, right bottom, are a fun couple at any swingin' soiree. The tortoise moves its head in and out of its shell, and the flamingo dips its head and raises its wings. Place them poolside, next to the patio, or in the middle of the yard.

Available at Michaels:
Dragonfly, flower, and frog lights • Lighted tortoise and flamingo • Bamboo torches • Glass ball lights

CREATIVE IDEA

Party lights can be the perfect antidote to any backyard blues. Even the plainest, tiniest, or unlikeliest corner of the yard can come alive with a string of sparkle. Attractive glass balls, like the one shown above, can be the starting point for the rest of your party's theme. Coordinate colors with paper goods or linens. Use other lights, too: scatter tea lights, votive candles, or torches along a pathway, and bring a candelabra outside to add drama to the picnic table.

8

decorative baskets

Few garden-style items are as versatile as good, sturdy decorative baskets. What other type of container would you reach for to hold a group of potted plants, a bunch of silk flowers, or a bouquet of fresh-cut flowers from the garden? You can also fill baskets with pine cones and evergreen boughs to create a colorful display for the front porch during the cold-weather months. And there is no end to the way baskets can be used indoors. Place a small basket near the front door to hold keys, wallets, and mail. Pile fresh fruit in a round or square basket to create a casual centerpiece for the breakfast table. In the bedroom, use baskets to store sweaters and socks. Decorative baskets are great for holding linens and towels in the bathroom. The next time you visit a friend, pack cookies, cupcakes, or some other treat in an oval or square basket with a handle. Leave the goodies and the basket as a thoughtful gift. Only your imagination limits the possibilities.

Baskets play a part in dozens of home projects.

Design Hint

Baskets have a homey appeal when left natural, but you can turn them into colorful accents when needed. Either fill them with brightly colored plants, or spray paint them any color you wish. Spray paint will do a better job of getting into the nooks than painting with a brush. Just be sure to protect any surrounding areas from overspray. If the baskets are exposed to the weather, the paint will wear off, leaving a popular distressed look.

Decorate porches and patios, opposite, with an assortment of baskets. Use them to hold potted plants so that you can move the arrangement around to change the look or take advantage of the sun.

The built-in handles on the basket above are usually found on baskets with tight weaves. Large-weave baskets, above right and right, have overhead handles.

Available at Michaels: ***White grapevine woven baskets with and without handles • Metal plant stand • Metal buckets (planters) • Clay pots • Hanging metal plant holder • Plaster-look cross • Faux-stone resin urn • Tight-weave basket with built-in handle • Galvanized watering can with weathered finish • Grapevine woven baskets • Butterfly and ladybug picks • Silk flowers***

Open shelving, left, lets you stow your stuff out of the way and puts your baskets on display.

Small baskets, below, are good for personal items.

Store linens and extra pillows in baskets in the bedroom, opposite.

Available at Michaels: ***All baskets on stand*** • ***Large baskets on floor*** • ***Light-tan baskets*** • ***Metal container***

INDOOR BASKETS

Baskets are useful in the garden, but they are almost indispensible inside the house. You can certainly use baskets with a coarse weave, but for many applications inside, consider smaller-weave baskets because they tend to have a more finished appearance and blend easily with a number of decorating styles. Select multiple sizes and shapes for your storage needs. You will not only have a place for everything, but you will also enhance the look of your home.

Design Hint

Fill a small basket with your favorite scented soaps. The different colors and sizes make a nice display, and the soaps will be handy when you want to use them. You can also fill a basket with potpourri or dried lavender, but make sure that the basket has a tight weave to avoid spills.

Master bathrooms, left, are great locations for all sorts of baskets because they can usually stand up to the humid conditions without losing their looks or shape. Select large baskets to serve as hampers as shown. Stack baskets of varying sizes on shelves to hold soaps, makeup, and other toiletries. Fill large square or rectangular baskets with towels and washcloths.

Use baskets in kids' rooms, above right, to help organize toys and games. You will find them to be a lifesaver for keeping track of toys with many small pieces.

Available at Michaels: ***Baskets on open shelves* • *Laundry hamper* • *Metal container* • *Clay pot* • *Silk flowers* • *Small oval and rectangular tan baskets***

CREATIVE IDEA

To make an overnight guest feel welcome, pack a small basket with soaps, shampoo, bath salts, and anything else—including a snack—you think that they might like, and place it on the bedside table. Round out the presentation with accessories that give the basket a theme, such as the shells shown here.

A Division of Federal Marketing Corp.
Upper Saddle River, NJ

Editorial Director Timothy O. Bakke
Production Manager Kimberly H. Vivas

Senior Editors Fran J. Donegan, Kathie Robitz
Assistant Editor Sharon Ranftle
Editorial Assistant Jennifer Ramcke

Senior Designers Glee Barre, David Geer
Photographer Spectra Studios, David Freeman
Photo Stylist Martha Shultz

Manufactured in the United States of America

Current Printing (last digit)
10 9 8 7 6 5 4 3 2 1

Michaels Garden Style
Library of Congress Control Number: 2002116155
ISBN: 1-58011-146-7

CREATIVE HOMEOWNER®
A Division of Federal Marketing Corp.
24 Park Way, Upper Saddle River, NJ 07458
www.creativehomeowner.com